Architectural Details
from Victorian Homes

by Stanley Schuler

4880 Lower Valley Road, Atglen, PA 19310 USA

Photographs by Miranda Burnett, Katherine Hull, Peter Lund, Al Malpa, and Stanley Schuler

Library of Congress Cataloging-in-Publication Data

Schuler, Stanley.
 Architectural details from Victorian homes / by Stanley Schuler.
    p. cm.
ISBN 0-7643-1829-2 (hardcover)
1. Architecture, Victorian--United States. 2. Architecture, Domestic--United States. 3. Architecture--Details.
I. Title.
NA7207.S34 2003
728'.37'097309034--dc21

2003008373

Designed by Joseph M. Riggio Jr.
Type set in Times New Roman

ISBN: 0-7643-1829-2
Printed in China

Published by Schiffer Publishing Ltd.
4880 Lower Valley Road
Atglen, PA 19310
Phone: (610) 593-1777; Fax: (610) 593-2002
E-mail: Info@schifferbooks.com
Please visit our web site catalog at
www.schifferbooks.com
We are always looking for people to write books on new and related subjects. If you have an idea for a book please contact us at the above address.

This book may be purchased from the publisher.
Include $3.95 for shipping.
Please try your bookstore first.
You may write for a free catalog.

In Europe, Schiffer books are distributed by
Bushwood Books
6 Marksbury Ave.
Kew Gardens
Surrey TW9 4JF England
Phone: 44 (0)20-8392-8585
Fax: 44 (0)20-8392-9876
E-mail: Bushwd@aol.com
Free postage in the UK. Europe: air mail at cost

Contents

Chapter 1

Introduction

After remodeling three houses, Charles and Janet Irving decided to build one for themselves on land that had once been used as a shipyard in Essex, Connecticut. It was to be a Victorian—one that the Victorians of the 1800s would have been proud of, but with all the modern amenities and, of course, meeting the local codes.

Given a good set of plans by someone who knows what Victorian houses were like, almost anyone can put up a Victorian home in about the same time that you can build, say, a Colonial. But Charles, a lawyer, loves architecture and building. He and Janet took about five years to complete plans for the house and another three years to build it. The long wait, a result of the determination and effort that went into the project, paid off. The house is outstanding in every detail.

It is a splendid lesson for anyone who wants not just an average Victorian house—the most common kind—but a home worthy of the old queen herself.

The Irving house is a three-story Italianate structure on the edge of Essex's historic North Cove. It has nine rooms, an entrance hall that in true Victorian fashion is approximately as large as the average guest room, an attic area that can be converted into three large bedrooms and baths, and a belvedere.

Charles and Janet based the plan in part on a historic Victorian in Rhinebeck, New York, though Charles takes most of the credit for it. Originally, this called for a mansard roof, but when he went before the Essex authorities for permission to build, he was turned down because the house exceeded the height allowed near the waterfront. So what had been planned as a Second Empire house was turned into an Italianate design with an almost flat roof supporting an unusually big and elaborate belvedere. This received the town's approval.

The house lies at a bend in the road and even though it is the largest edifice in the immediate neighborhood, you are not aware of it until you are directly in front of it. You are then immediately struck by its size—although it does not cover an exceptionally large piece of ground—how different it is from its colonial neighbors, and its detailing, ranging from the ornate portico protecting the double-leaved front door, to the windows with their neatly trimmed drip-guards, to the very wide eaves supported by handsome large brackets.

The façade prepares you for the interior, but only partially, since it is more typical of the Deep South than New England. Despite the large, tall windows overlooking the cove, the rooms are not bright. This is because the decorative scheme, as in most big Victorian and Southern residences, is rich, warm, and subdued.

Victorian architecture came into being because the people of that era were tired of the stiff, cold look of the classic style preceding it. They wanted something warmer and romantic, and the Victorian style that evolved filled the bill in every way. Charles and Janet achieved this in their new home, not with modern materials finished in paint but with the actual materials of the 1800s. These, of course, took time to accumulate, but it was time well spent because it largely accounts for the calm beauty of the house.

Except for the materials that went into the basic structure—the concrete of the underpinnings, the studs and joists, the plywood sheathing, wiring, copper tubing, etc.—the finish materials are in large part old, dating back a century or more. Surprisingly, junkyards were not the principal source of these. Charles and Janet got them by advertising in publications read by people interested in antiques and collecting. For instance, their most productive haul resulted from an ad they ran in an antiques quarterly asking for materials that came from or might have come from early Victorian structures. Every morning after the ad appeared, they waited eagerly to see what the mail would bring. Then a letter arrived from a woman in Iowa saying she had owned two Victorian houses and had taken one of them down. Now she had an enormous collection of things she would be happy to sell.

Charles wasted little time in replying that he would come to Iowa at once. It was a trip well worth the time and expense because it yielded most of the interior materials the Irvings were looking for and they weren't cut from pine or fir. It was a beautiful butternut not only of exceptional thickness but also in lengths required for a house with 12-foot ceilings. There were also handsome pocket doors to close off the parlor from the living room and the living room from the front hall, hardware, lighting fixtures, etc.

Once Charles had struck a deal with the woman, he rented a large trailer and drove the treasure trove back to Essex.

There are other finish materials in the house that are antique. These include a marble fireplace once meant for a Newport, Rhode Island, mansion; a bronze gas-fired chandelier rumored to have hung in the White House; and a red-and-green-veined marble fireplace from an ancient house in New London, Connecticut.

So many Americans today are remodeling old houses of all styles or building modern replicas that many businesses have sprung up to collect or reproduce the old materials and components required. In San Francisco, for examples, San Francisco Victorians, Inc. has been in business for thirty-two years selling materials it produces or salvages to people who are renovating or building Victorian homes. In its 190-page catalog, the company illustrates the most common styles of wood moldings and plaster castings used in Victorian houses in the San Francisco Bay area since 1850. In addition to manufacturing and stocking several hundred of these moldings, it also makes custom reproductions for any project requiring a unique item.

A number of similar firms scattered around the country make reproductions of period moldings, ceiling centerpieces, lighting fixtures, and even old toilets with wooden tanks that hang high on the wall above the bowl.

Just about the only antique building components that are hard to come by are reproductions of early hardware items, but the gap is being fast filled.

Besides the companies that stock reproductions of old building components, there is no dearth of craftsmen who are able to turn out excellent substitutes for hard-to-find materials. Because nineteenth century kitchens bear no resemblance to those of today, the Irvings, for example, turned to a cabinetmaker in a nearby small town to create theirs in walnut. And when they got around to finishing the interior of the house, they hired a contractor who specializes in rebuilding old houses and constructing modern copies.

Obviously, the Irvings' house is not a run-of-the-mill structure. On the contrary, it compares—if not in size, at least in beauty—with the famed Mark Twain house in Hartford, Connecticut, or the Storrs house across the street; with Lyndhurst in Tarrytown, New York; Longwood in Natchez, Mississippi; Kingscote in Newport, Rhode Island; the Rotch house in New Bedford, Massachusetts; the Davies Mansion in New Haven; and the innumerable Vanderbilt mansions.

Many of the great houses of the Victorian era have, for one reason or another, been razed, but many still exist, mostly in cities, some in rural areas. When the average person speaks of Victorian houses, these are the edifices he or she is thinking about.

But the smaller, simpler Victorians are in far greater numbers. On Martha's Vineyard alone, in the small community of Oak Bluffs, 312 diminutive Victorians are crammed into a 34-acre enclave measuring about 2,750 feet long by 1,000 feet wide. Started in the nineteenth century as a religious tent colony, the canvas shelters slowly gave way to tiny houses with steep roofs and gables, pointed church windows, imaginative gingerbread, and brilliant paint jobs.

Not many neighborhoods have smaller or more colorful Victorian houses, but in numerous areas modest-sized homes of Victorian design exist and they are just as fascinating today as they were when built.

Gingerbread, towers, encircling porches, balconies, odd mixtures of materials, large porte-cocheres, bay windows, elaborate chimneys—at no time in the history of architecture did architects, builders, and homeowners let their imaginations run so wild.

As a result, Victorian houses were looked on for much of the last century with derision. But in recent years, after a long period of unimaginative architecture or what many people consider downright ugly architecture, the Victorian style is staging a comeback.

At first glance, the Irving house is striking for its size and beauty. On closer examination, you're amazed by the great variety of its details. Despite its unusual size, the belvedere is set back so far from the roof edges that you cannot see how ornate it really is.

This large portico gives excellent protection against rain and snow except when it is driving in almost horizontally from the cove beyond. Ornamental ironwork, which is also used on the roof of the belvedere, was a feature of many old Victorians, but most of it is now gone.

The two-leaf front door opens into a large vestibule. The thick glass is etched.

The side door opens onto the porch that goes around much of the back of the house. It also has etched glass.

A second door separates the vestibule from the large front hall. The vestibule floor is marble tile.

Very wide roof overhangs are supported by
intricately cut brackets spaced several feet apart.

Windows throughout the house vary. These, on the
water side, extend from the floor to about 7 feet and
have semi-rounded tops.

The bay window also faces the water. Slender double windows on the second floor are partially framed by ornate drip caps.

Despite their efforts to build a perfect replica of an antique Victorian house, the Irvings did not forget they were building a modern house, and they installed all possible modern conveniences and took full advantage of their water view.

Sunlight streams through the bay window into the living room on the east side of the house overlooking the cove off the Connecticut River.

Victorian homeowners had a liking for stained glass, although in many cases they would use it in small pieces, often in bands around clear-glass windows. The Irvings had this large stained-glass window specially made.

The large stained glass window on the west side of the house floods the interior with colored light in the late afternoon.

Another stained glass window. As in all such windows, the colors change with the outdoor light. The blue in the background of this window is actually much darker than it appears.

Triple stained glass windows help to light the main stairway, which is also lighted by three electric fixtures, starting with the globe on the newel post and including chandeliers hanging from the first- and second-story ceilings.

The Irvings found antique electric chandeliers hard to find, so most of those they installed are fairly new. Gas chandeliers, however, are more widely available.

Old ceiling medallions or centerpieces are also scarce, but modern copies made of plaster are much more available in round, oval, or square units. Elaborate plaster castings in ropes, ribbons, etc. are also available.

Fireplaces have always been the focal point of the rooms in which they are located, and this is the case in the Irving house. Large plate-glass mirrors were commonly set into the over-mantels.

Large houses in Victorian days were generally heated (but not well) by coal-burning fireplaces. Fireplaces in cities had gas logs or perhaps coal grates. Wood was burned outside the cities, as it is in the Irving house.

Lavatories and tubs from the Victorian era can still be found in junkyards, but they are generally smaller than those manufactured today.

The toilet in the powder room off the front hall looks like an antique, but it is actually new. It is made to meet modern plumbing codes.

Tall pocket doors came from a nineteenth century Victorian house in Iowa. Despite their size, they slide easily into and out of the recesses in the walls.

Hardwood door.

Cornices used in early Victorian homes were large. The size used by the Irvings depended on what they could find. But as a rule, the size is determined by the height of the ceiling. Wood is used for moldings that are easily run through machines. Plaster is used for complicated moldings.

Old bracket finished in gold leaf.

Embossed wallcoverings, also called anaglypta, were used in the front hall. The material is made of heavy wallpaper and embossed in various patterns. It is installed like ordinary wallpaper, then painted.

Chapter 2

Styles of Victorian Architecture

Just about anyone who is interested in architecture can recognize a Victorian house. The style was popular throughout Queen Victoria's reign from roughly 1840 to 1900. But it was not a simple style. It was, in fact, seven styles, or substyles, and some purists would like to break it down into even more substyles.

That would be carrying things too far because it would make for too much confusion. Seven substyles is enough, especially since there is considerable sameness between them.

In America, Victorian architecture captured the public's enthusiasm when people grew tired of the preceding Greek Revival style. The latter became the country's semiofficial architecture at the urging of Washington and Jefferson, who felt that the new country should have an architecture that expressed the strength, determination, and formality of a brave new world. Furthermore, they wanted to get rid of the Georgian and Federal styles that the country had inherited from the British. Greek Revival was different from both of these; it was formal and monumental, and it had great strength and vigor. But after about twenty years, despite the popularity of the two great Virginians, the American people decided they had had enough of the Greek Revival style's stiffness. They wanted something that was more fun, more romantic, and they switched to the Victorian style even though it was named for a British monarch.

The first of the Victorian substyles was known as Gothic Revival. Its foremost proponents were Andrew Jackson Davis, an architect, and Andrew Jackson Downing, a landscape architect who published Davis's plans for Gothic houses in his enormously popular landscaping books.

Davis's best-known house was Lyndhurst, a mansion near Tarrytown, New York, with a distinct resemblance to an elaborate medieval castle. But his most popular houses were much smaller structures like that illustrated on page 21. Most of these were of board-and-batten construction that emphasized the vertical. They had very steep roofs with steep cross gables, elaborate chimneys and extravagantly cut-out or carved bargeboards (also called vergeboards) on the gable ends.

The Italianate (sometimes called Tuscan) architectural style overlapped the Gothic but was most popular in the decade before the Civil War. Many examples remain today and, for the most part, are easily identified because they have very low-pitched roofs with wide overhanging eaves supported on prominent carved brackets. A small number of Italianate houses have square towers. More are crowned with belvederes that resemble cupolas but are large enough for one or more people to stand in. Windows throughout Italianate houses are usually tall and narrow and rounded at the top.

After the Italianate style came the Second Empire style, which was largely derived from France. It was more formal and monumental than any other Victorian style and is easily identified by its mansard roof. This is a double-pitched roof shaped like a capital L turned upside down with both legs on a slant. The lower longer leg is steeply slanted and often has dormer windows set into it; the upper leg is on a slight slant. Whether a mansard roof is used on a one-story house or a much taller structure like the Old Executive Office Building in Washington, D.C., it gives the building a distinctive flair and makes it possible to walk around in the attic under the roof without stooping.

Other features of Second Empire houses are the pavilions (short wings) on the sides of the building and the columns or pilasters that often support pediments over windows and doors.

Unfortunately, the Second Empire style was too formal for the average homeowner, with the result that it was used mainly by the wealthy and for nonresidential buildings. So the Victorian styles that followed in the last third of the nineteenth century were, for the most part, simpler.

The one exception was the Richardsonian Romanesque style developed by Henry Hobson Richardson, one of the greatest American architects. Richardson designed only a few houses, and his followers did likewise. This was because his style looked too massive and heavy for anything except a huge residence. He built mainly with stone—often very big blocks of stone—and made much use of large rounded arches over doors and windows that were set in deep openings. Unlike most Victorian buildings, which had a distinctly vertical appearance, Richardson's buildings were horizontal, and while they repeated various Victorian features, they somehow lacked the Victorian's light charm.

The Romanesque substyle was followed by the aptly named Shingle Style, the strange and strangely named Stick Style, and the very popular Queen Anne Style.

The Shingle Style was particularly popular in the Northeast close to the seashore. Houses are clad almost entirely with wood shingles that are allowed to weather a natural gray. Even porch columns are covered with wood shingles. Whatever exterior woodwork was used was quite simple. But from a distance, a Shingle Style house, despite its basic simplicity, often looks surprisingly like a much more complicated Queen Anne house.

This is also true of Stick Style houses. In general appearance they are much like Queen Anne houses. They got their strange name from the ornamentation achieved with plain boards or timbers. For instance, a common feature is the trusses tucked under the steep gables and cross gables. In the Queen Anne or Gothic substyles, where similar trusses are often used, they tended to be quite ornate. But in Stick Style houses, the trusses more often look as if they had been put together by an ordinary carpenter to support the roof. The braces at the top of porch columns also look like ordinary supports rather than lacy valentines.

On the other hand, the sticks that are the features of exterior walls have no counterparts in other Victorian houses. They are plain boards applied vertically, horizontally, or diagonally over the siding to form a pattern. The result is somewhat like the pattern formed by the large exposed timbers in English Tudor buildings, but on close examination, you can see the boards overlaying the siding instead of being flush with it.

Queen Anne architecture has little connection with the architecture of the early Queen Anne period. But it was extremely popular; there are probably more American houses of this style than of any other Victorian style. In shape the Queen Anne house was very complex, with numerous roofs and roof levels; large porches that often extend around two or three sides of a house; and unusually lovely railings, columns, and friezes called spindlework. A round or polygonal tower was often placed at a front corner of the house. Exterior walls were clad with contrasting materials (say, shingles and clapboards) at different levels. Gable fronts might be elaborately ornamented.

A Queen Anne house, in other words, is very decorative—nothing like our early Colonial houses or even our handsome Georgian houses. Among American houses, the nearest thing to them are the large complex residences that are so popular among developers and buyers today.

This house by Andrew Jackson Davis was built in Old Lyme, Connecticut, in 1844, and from the front, it looks almost exactly as it did then. The main change was made in the steps, which originally ran around the front and sides of the porch. Though the house looks small, it is actually quite spacious and has 12-foot ceilings on the first floor. Surprisingly, it has horizontal board siding; most of Davis's houses used vertical boards.

Gothic architecture was sometimes very elaborate. This was especially true of large houses like this one in St. Francisville, Louisiana. *Photo from the Collections of the Library of Congress.*

Typical Gothic houses in (left) Portland, Maine and (right) Windsor, Vermont. Like most Gothic houses, they have steep roofs and very steep gables centered on the façade; elaborate gingerbread on the bargeboards; and narrow double windows with pointed arches.

The Italianate houses that overlapped the Gothic were at first glance simpler, but many of them, like the one above in Memphis, Tennessee, had very ornate features. Prominent brackets support the wide eaves, and the long narrow windows with slightly rounded tops have elaborate drip caps that serve the practical purpose of carrying rainwater around the windows.

Another Italianate house, this one in Little Rock, Arkansas. The brackets are not as prominent as those on the Memphis house, but the roof does not appear as large or heavy. The windows have the same slightly arched tops but are a little wider. The bay window is topped by fancy ironwork.

The architect and owner of the Jerome Bonaparte Pillow House in Helena, Arkansas, must have worked overtime to make this large house stand out from its neighbors. It has three towers, numerous gables, elaborate spindlework in the friezes under the porch roofs, a fancy chimney, and stickwork in the gable in the front of the house, and more stickwork in the truncated gable on the left side.

The Fontaine house, a Second Empire design, is one of the showplaces of Memphis. A similar large house is around the street corner to the right. Both have square towers that rise high above the mansard roofs. Note that the roof here is patterned—made of rounded slates inlaid with dark-colored slates in diamond patterns. The brackets and porch columns are uniquely shaped and the heavy masonry drip caps over the arched second-floor windows and the windows in the tower differ from window to window.

Compared with most of the mansions in Newport, Rhode Island, this equally large house looks like what it really is—a summer cottage built in the Shingle substyle. But it differs from other Shingle-substyle houses in one respect: the porch columns are not sheathed with shingles.

Stickwork in a Stick-substyle house in Old Saybrook, Connecticut. To add interest to the front of the gable, six-inch boards are applied over the shingle siding.

Chapter 3
Towers

Although Victorian houses are known for their fanciful foibles and intricacies, they widely share only two unusual features—their gingerbread and their towers.

Gingerbread of one kind or another is seen in almost all Victorian house styles. Towers are not so common. In their *Field Guide to American Houses,* Virginia and Lee McAlester estimate that as many as 75 percent of all Richardsonian Romanesque houses have towers. But such a high figure cannot be applied to other Victorian substyles. The McAlesters estimate, for example, that only 15 percent of Italianate houses have towers, while 30 percent of Second Empire houses have them.

Even so, towers are so unusual on American houses, and they take up so much space horizontally and vertically, that they appear more common than they really are.

What is it that makes them so beguiling? The fact that you almost never see them on other styles of house—that they are strictly a Victorian phenomenon—is one reason for making people like them. But a more important reason is that they instantly bring to mind the long-ago days when they were more com-

mon—on large houses, at least—than they are today.

Towers bring to mind the times of the Crusades and the hugely popular novels of Sir Walter Scott. Towers are of a romantic era. And even in this tough, difficult twenty-first century, almost all of us have a romantic streak.

Many of the towers on Victorian houses are too simple and plain to inspire a romantic feeling in the viewer. But many others are quite the opposite. You can find plain and handsome towers on houses of all Victorian styles. Some of the towers are round, some are square, and some are polygonal. Some are slender and rise high above the main roof of the house they grace; some are squat and make you wonder if you should really call them towers. Some are elaborately ornamental; some are crowned by fancy and fanciful cast iron cresting; some have flat roofs; some have domed roofs. Some towers bulge out from the house; some are centered on the façade; some are squeezed into a front corner. There are even houses that have two large towers.

The towers on Victorian houses are unique. And they add immeasurably to Victorian residential architecture.

Chapter 4
Gingerbread

Considering how often architectural gingerbread is referred to, it is surprising how little we know about how and why it came into use. I have checked every possible reference book my library has and only one—the Oxford Dictionary—offers any clues to the answer.

We know what gingerbread is in a general sort of way. But what exactly does the word mean? And what is its derivation. Even the Oxford Dictionary fails us here.

The dictionary says that first use of the word in writing was made in 1748. "Gingerbread work," the book says, was "originally applied by sailors to the carved and gilded decorations of a ship; hence to architectural or other ornament of a gaudy and tasteless kind."

But what is this gaudy and tasteless work?

The general assumption is that it is the fancy carved wood that hangs from the edges of gables and roofs. In architectural terms, these are bargeboards or vergeboards. Some of this carved wood looks more or less like heavy rope hanging in loops. Some resembles a row of darts or eyeteeth. Some forms the fringe of a long porch roof or the edge of a window canopy.

One of the most common uses of gingerbread—even on houses that have no other decoration of this sort—is in the roughly triangular braces that connect porch columns to the porch roof. In other houses, the braces are extended into friezes connecting several porch columns one to the other. Going one step far-

ther, many builders extended the friezes down the columns and across the porch floor, thus turning the usual rectangular openings between columns into fat tomato shapes.

The railings on porches often play an important role in the gingerbread on houses. In these cases, the balusters lose their traditional shapes and are treated in more imaginative fashion. Sometimes they are made into cutouts of people (see the picture in which the second floor railing is made up of a row of gingerbread men). Sometimes they form a line of geometric figures. Frequently, they are simple, straight, slender spindles placed close together. Spindlework is the name given gingerbread of this kind.

The ornamental braces used in gable peaks are still another kind of gingerbread. In general outline—which is roughly triangular—these resemble the simple braces used in Stick Style houses. But they are far more complex and lovely, usually including a graceful finial that rises above the gable peak.

Most of the ornament that is popularly known as gingerbread is scrollwork and owes its start in the earliest Gothic houses and widespread use thereafter to the invention of the jigsaw. But lacking a precise definition to the contrary, gingerbread is not limited to open work. In the past, when many of the materials for Victorian houses came out of factories, gingerbread was often produced by gluing factory-made buttons, rosebuds, and other ornaments to flat boards. Decorations were also incised or carved in wood.

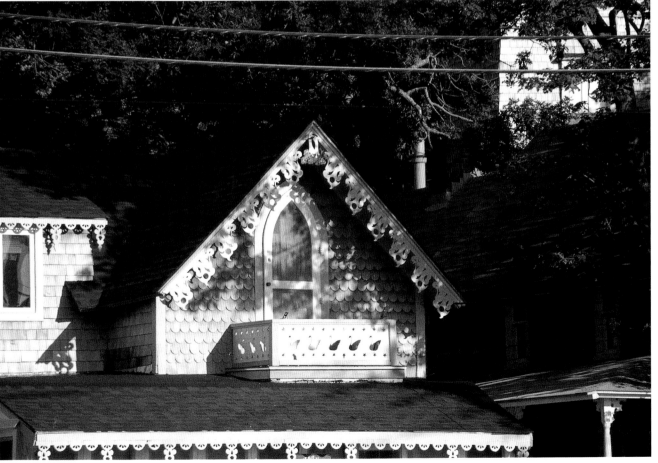

Chapter 5
Roofs and Chimneys

The roofs of Victorian houses are either almost flat and invisible or steep—sometimes very steep. Flat roofs are restricted to Italianate houses, but surprisingly they do not detract from the looks of such houses because they have two features that work in their favor.

One of these is the handsome brackets that support wide roof overhangs. The other is the belvedere rising from the center of the roof. Both of these charming architectural elements are used on other Victorian houses, but to a rather limited extent.

Pitched roofs are more common in Victorian architecture than flat roofs but have one drawback: They dominate the structure they cap because they cover such a large area. To compensate for this problem, architects and builders often resorted to the practice of covering roofs with slates or shingles in unusual shapes or in several colors laid in large patterns. The alternative was to reduce the apparent size of roofs by breaking a monotonous expanse with decorative cross gables and dormers.

When mansard roofs came into style, builders snatched at them not only to add interest to houses but also to create livable space in what had been not very useful attics. Mansard roofs generally were more attractive than ordinary pitched roofs because the lower section could be either concave or, less often, convex, and they could also be pierced by windows or dormers. Some mansards were also covered with slates or shingles in various shapes and colors.

Chimneys were also a decorative element of many roofs. This was especially true when a chimney had to be made large enough to carry several flues. These often were topped by fancy chimney pots, or the bricks in the chimneys were laid to create a sculptured geometrical texture.

Mansard Roofs

Belvederes

Brackets

Gables

Chimneys

119

121

Chapter 6
Windows

Although Victorian interiors tended to be dark because dark hardwoods, such as walnut, were favored for interior doors and woodwork, windows were large and numerous.

Why Victorians had such a love of windows I do not know. But they seemed to install them wherever there was a blank wall that, they thought, needed some sort of ornamentation.

And Victorian windows were very ornamental. This was, perhaps, a reaction on the part of homeowners to the simplicity of Colonial, Georgian, Federal, and Greek Revival windows. In large city houses up to about 1840, the windows were often handsome, but they were also similar. In Victorian houses, starting with the Gothic style, simple rectangular windows gave way to arched windows, and from there they took off. Windows appeared in various shapes. They were used not just singly but also in pairs and threes and even fours.

They also differed from early windows in dimensions. Whereas colonial windows tended to be shaped about like the standard window of today, Victorian windows were more often tall and narrow. This was undoubtedly because Victorian ceilings were high, rising to a height of 10 or 12 feet. So the windows grew to stay in good proportion.

The real charm of Victorian windows was in the elaborate manner in which they were framed. Simple casings of flat or grooved boards were used, especially in the later 1800s. But the really beautiful frames that enclosed the sashes are to be seen on Italianate and Second Empire houses. Of these, the most conspicuous were the drip caps that formed upside-down Us over the tops of the windows. These were called drip caps or drip molds or hood molds because they were not only used for ornament but also to carry rainwater running down the walls around the windows, thus restricting streaking to a certain extent.

Pediments and scalloped hoods like those used in many Georgian corner cupboards and shallow roofs of various designs supported on brackets were an alternative to drip caps. Although not as effective as caps in diverting water, they were equally handsome. They were used primarily on flat-topped windows.

Many windows were also completely framed from the sills on up.

Dormer windows received the same elaborate treatment. Occasionally this was overdone, but generally the dormers on Victorian houses are far handsomer than those on Georgian houses and certainly far more imaginative. One kind of dormer window, however, had little to offer either in appearance or practicality. This was known as an eyebrow window because that's almost exactly what it looked like: a half-open human eye with a curved wood brow.

Among this large collection of windows, there was one type that stood out—if not in numbers, certainly in size and popularity among Victorian homeowners. This was the bay window consisting usually of three sashes installed in a bay projecting about two or three feet from the wall of a house. Bay windows were so popular in San Francisco, which is famous for its array of Victorian residences, that some people call it "the city of bay windows."

Bays were not known for great beauty. Some, admittedly, were handsomely decorated. But their main purpose was to increase light and space and a view of the neighborhood from inside the house. The most common bays had three windows—one in the front and one on each side. Some bays had slanted sides; in others, the sides were at right angles to the front. There were also round bays with several window sashes; slanted bays without any side windows; and bays that rose from the ground to the eaves of the house.

One other fairly common feature of Victorian windows was the glass. Most of it was colorless but much was colored. Large stained glass windows that rivaled those in churches (though of a secular nature) adorned many of the homes of the wealthy. Windows composed of numerous small rectangles or diamond-shaped panes of several colors were popular among the less well-to-do. Probably the most prevalent kind of stained glass window was a conventional rectangular sash in which the large central colorless glass was surrounded by a row of small squares of red, blue, yellow, etc. glass.

125

127

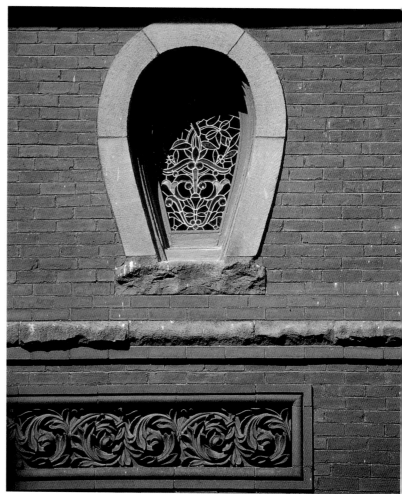

Bay Windows

Dormers

Chapter 7
Porches and Entrances

The first thing that usually comes to mind when Victorian houses are under discussion is their appearance. But their plan is, of course, more important. My youngest daughter owned a very attractive Queen Anne house, but as proud as she and her family were of its appearance, it was the layout of the house that sold her on it in the first place and kept her happy in it for twenty years after that.

Up to the time Victorian houses became popular in the United States, the standard American house was a rectangle with two rooms in front and two in back, and heating was done by large fireplaces—usually three in the middle of the house venting into a single central chimney. Framing of the house was done with a large post at each outside corner connected by girts at the tops of the posts.

But about 1830, home building and plans changed radically. Balloon framing done with 2x4s came into use, and heating began to be done with stoves vented into small chimneys or metal stovepipes. The two changes greatly simplified construction and the standard rectangular house gave way to a much less rigid plan. Now builders and homeowners were free to locate rooms wherever they wanted and there was no real limit, except money, on their size. One of the favorite changes—improvements, if you prefer—made by the freewheeling Victorians was to project one of the front rooms forward from the main body of the house. Then they filled in the resulting empty space with a porch or perhaps two porches, one on either side of the projecting room.

Most porches, of course, were small. But some were enormous, stretching across the front of the house and around the corners at one or both ends. Then for no apparent reason—perhaps for show; perhaps because they really couldn't get enough of the outdoors; or perhaps, if they lived in the South, to shade the bedrooms from the hot afternoon sun—they added second-story porches or, sometimes, only balconies.

However many porches they built, everyone used them to add more decorative flourishes to the house.

All porches required railings to keep people from falling off the edge. But not just ordinary railings. Railings should be pretty and imaginative—and they were.

Porches also needed posts to support the porch roofs. Here were more opportunities for ornamentation, and butterfly-like braces were created to connect them to the roofs. Lacy friezes were often hung between the tops of columns.

Circular or oval frames divided large openings between columns into valentines or fans like the ladies used to keep cool on hot days.

The porches on Victorian houses were sometimes the most creative, most charming aspects of the houses. Much of this decoration was spindlework—lengths of wood delicately turned on lathes and then frequently placed close together in the railings and friezes.

Except in cities, where front doors opened more or less directly onto the street, most of the front doors in Victorian houses opened onto the porches. In larger houses, where porches were likely to be relegated to the sides or back of the dwelling, however, front doors opened on to handsome porticoes with large columns, often clustered, supporting segmental arches and, above these, flat roofs edged with slender lovely ironwork.

After all, Victorians were proud of their home, and the best way to show them off was to welcome visitors handsomely at the front door.

Porches

Second Story Porches

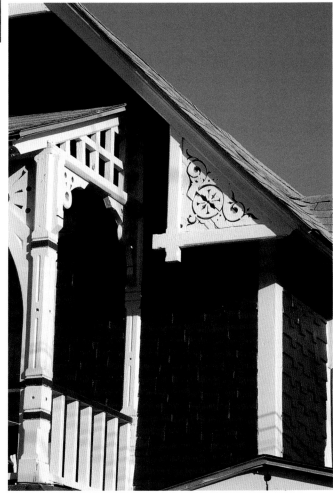

Entrances

Chapter 8
Siding

The Victorian house's principal exterior wall surfaces were really no more ornamental than those of any other architectural style. You just didn't notice them very much because the house offered so many distractions. If a house was masonry, the walls were conventional brick or stone laid in horizontal courses. If the house was clad in wood, the walls were commonly made of vertical boards and battens during the Gothic era. Thereafter, the walls were made of horizontal boards usually with beaded edges. Such relatively plain, smooth surfaces were the ideal background for the fanciness of the trim, etc.

The principal effort to draw attention to the exterior walls was made in the Queen Anne and Stick substyles. In houses of the former style, patterned shingles were used with abandon—especially in the large gables. The shingles were fashioned in an astonishing array of shapes that were either used alone or in strips. The same effects were achieved in masonry houses by laying bricks in different bands—say, several courses in a running band alternating with several courses of a basketweave—or different textures or colors. Sometimes, colored or textured tiles were inserted.

In houses of the Stick substyle, the boards in the walls were laid in alternating vertical and horizontal positions. Or smooth wall surfaces were overlaid with boards laid singly in vertical, horizontal, or diagonal strips more or less in the way that the studs hidden in the walls were used.

The use of paint in many bright hues to decorate house walls goes back to about 1880. Even though a great many houses were—and still are—just white or gray or brownish yellow, Victorians loved color. Witness the collection of brightly painted little houses at Oak Bluffs on Martha's Vineyard. Or the Charles R. Hart House shown on the next pages that was painted ten different colors—"earth tones," the owner says, ranging from browns to rusty reds to blues at the top, "taking your eye to the sky."

Board and Batten

Mixed Siding

Shingle

Stickwork

Paint

Chapter 9
Interior Details

When it came to lavishing attention on the exteriors of Victorian homes, builders did as well by small inexpensive houses as they did by large. After all, the big market for Victorian houses in the 1800s was among people of low and modest incomes, and the way to attract them to the homes being built was to overload the building with eye-catching details, such as lots of gingerbread and bay windows and turrets. Fancy interior treatment was less important.

But people with high incomes were more demanding. They wanted good planning and detailing inside as well as—perhaps even more than—outside. The result is that the most interesting decoration is found in the Victorian houses that were designed by architects for people with money.

The following abbreviated description of one of these large houses was written by Lewis A. Storrs, Jr., the son of Mrs. Zalmon Austin Storrs of Hartford, Connecticut in 1898 after his father's death. The architect was Isaac Allen of Hartford. A number of the photographs in this chapter are of the home.

"It contains 20 rooms plus pantries and storage space on three floors, a large attic on the fourth floor and a full basement," Lewis Storrs wrote. "Isaac Allen designed a handsome and liveable house. The style was eclectic. There were classical balustrades and columns, while the bargeboards and the metal crenallations atop the ridges were based on English Tudor residential architecture. The exterior walls were solid brick, 12 inches thick, with the face brick a white local brick. The foundations were brownstone ashlar. The entrance steps, lintels, door and windowsill and chimney caps were also brownstone. The gable ends were wood shingles and the roof red slate. The windows were wood, double-hung, with single sheets of plate glass in the important rooms. There were a few small windows with decorative leaded panes.

"You entered the house up a broad flight of brownstone steps, crossed a spacious wooden veranda to a vestibule, then entered the front hall which led to the broad, main stairs. To the left was a side wall leading to another vestibule and the porte cochere. At the front on the left was the parlor; behind the side hall, a sitting room, called the Turkish or Japanese room because of a stencil design on the ceiling and a sofa with a heavy canopy. On the right was the library and behind it the dining room. The hall and all these rooms were richly detailed with wide bases and cornices and paneling. They all had fireplaces, with elaborate mantels, many with beveled mirrors over them, all different but quite handsome. The halls, Turkish room and dining room were trimmed in quartered oak, the library in mahogany while the parlor was pine painted. The large and cheerful dining room was paneled in oak up to a plate rail. There were built-in cabinets for china and silver. All the rooms had chandeliers, the one in the dining room being the shape of a deep dome of rose-colored glass with beaded fringe along the bottom. Double sliding doors were between the rooms and the halls and between the library and dining room, which opened up the whole downstairs.

"The front stairs were oak with paneled wainscots, fretwork and decorative posts, rails and balusters. On the landing part way up was a built-in seat under a large window.

"According to today's standards, toilet and bathing facilities were far from satisfactory. Mrs. Storrs had a white tile private bath adjoining her bedroom with a marble lavatory with metal legs, a freestanding bathtub with claw feet, a foot tub and a water closet. The rest of the family used a white tile bathroom off the second floor hall. A passage from the hall to Mr. and Mrs. Storrs' bedroom contained a marble lavatory. In a dark closet off of it was a water closet. There was a lavatory and water closet off the first floor hall, a counterpart of today's powder room, but much less elegant. The servants had a bathtub and water closet off the third floor rear hall. Nearby in a closet was a slop sink which served as their lavatory.

"Closet space was quite inadequate. Hanging rods and coat hangers don't seem to have been thought of. The bedroom closets were narrow and deep with built-in drawers at the back in several of them. The coat closet was under the front stairs, but the door averaged five feet high. Consequently, coats were hung on a coat rack and on hooks at the side of a framed mirror in the side hall.

"In 1900 electricity was being installed in most buildings, but there was not complete confidence in it. Practically all the lighting fixtures in the Storrs house had both electric and gas outlets, but it was very seldom that the gas had to be resorted to. However, this combination made for some interesting fixtures. The gas outlet might be surrounded by bowl-shaped decorative glass shades. A chandelier might have four or five above or outside the electrical outlets. Sometimes simulated candles were used."

The one thing Mr. Storrs neglected in this description of the house, which is now occupied by charitable organizations but kept in almost the same condition in which they found it, was a description of the amazing manner in which the handsome hardwood woodwork was carved or adorned with small wooden sculptures. Similarly, many of the ceilings have plaster medallions and ornaments, cast and painted like ribbons, flowers, etc. Such embellishment of the Storrs house was common among most Victorian houses like it.

For instance, in a description of the Charles R. Hart House in Windsor, Connecticut, the *Hartford Daily Times* in 1896 reported that the house "is finished throughout in quartered oak, cherry and white wood. There are fourteen rooms in the building, six being used as chambers. The parlor, reception and dining rooms and the library are finished in cherry. In the library the mantel and fireplace add to the surroundings, and the decorations throughout the house are of the loveliest character. Quartered oak and cherry are used in finishing the chambers. There is a handsome billiard room in the tower division, which will be used by Mr. Hart in entertaining his guests from the city. The veranda fronts on the main street and also the south. Mr. Hart has had an electric gas lighting plant established for making gas. The tanks are on the outside, being practically concealed beneath the surface of the ground. A complete city system of plumbing has been introduced and every facility for comfort and enjoyment will be had that is accessible in the municipality."

In the 1980s the house was restored as a bed and breakfast, named the Charles R. Hart House. The present owners have updated it but made relatively few changes.

Fireplace with ceramic tile surround.

Dining room fireplace with a typically handsome mantel.

Same fireplace has a heavy iron fireback resembling a lion.

Unusual fireplace extends about two feet into large front hall.

Plate-glass mirror in the elaborate overmantel of a parlor fireplace.

Ornately carved mantel.

Brightly polished mahogany above a mirror overmantel.

Arched pediment above a mirror overmantel.

Fireplace breast is bordered on both sides by double columns.

More carving on a mantel.

Small bracket supports cornice above a fireplace mantel.

Bowed mantel seems to be supported by carved figure.

Typical 19th century carving.

Stairs generally were less handsome in Victorian homes than in Georgian residences of an earlier era.

Victorians didn't waste space if they could help it. Notice low closet under staircase at left.

In this picture and the next slender
balusters support stair railing.

Top of newel post in preceding photo.

Spirally cut newel post was more typical of Georgian architecture.

Top of spiral newel post.

Even the brackets under the stair treads were elaborately carved. (These brackets carry no weight and are just ornamental.)

Victorians depended largely on hanging crystal or glass chandeliers for lighting formal rooms.

Electric wall lights.

When houses were first electrified about the end of the 1800s, electricity wasn't considered entirely trustworthy, so early lighting fixtures worked on both electricity and gas.

Unusual stained glass window.

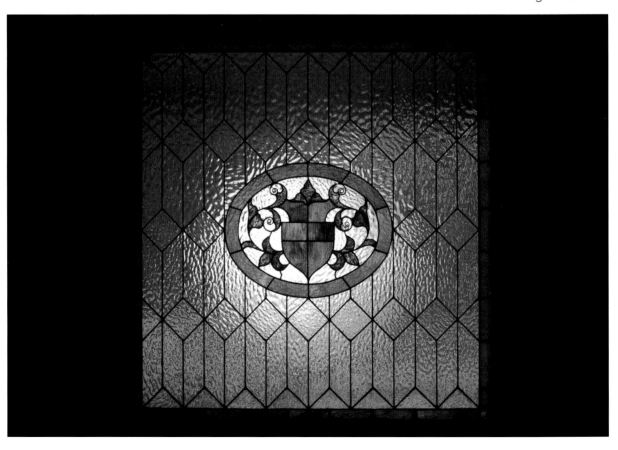

Fanlight over door between front vestibule and front hall.

Rectangular transom light between vestibule and front hall.

In Victorian houses, ceiling decoration was as important as that on walls. Most of it was much more delicate than this, however.

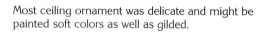

Most ceiling ornament was delicate and might be painted soft colors as well as gilded.

Another example of ceiling decoration. The ribbons, bows, etc. were molded in plaster before they were applied.

Handsome wide wallpaper borders topped papered rooms.

The gold moldings dividing wallpaper from borders
were made in plaster before application.

The walls of the stairway and entrance hall in the
Charles R. Hart House are still covered with the original
Lincrusta wallcoverings.

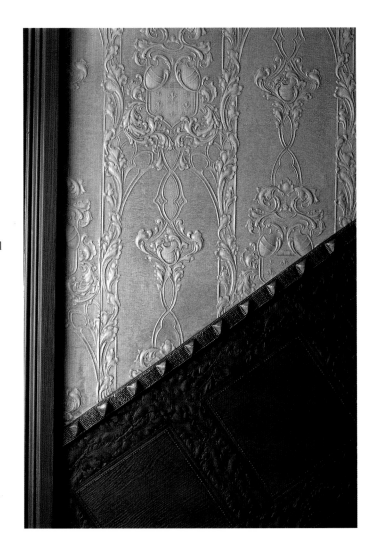

Victorians often built their sideboards into the walls instead
of using freestanding furniture pieces. Built-ins also included
bookcases, dumbwaiters (hidden within the walls), etc.

Carved and elaborately shaped woodwork was not
limited to fireplaces, paneled walls, wainscots,
cornices. Anything made of beautiful hardwoods
might be carved, too, as in the last six pictures here.
(Shown on this and following pages.)

9 780764 318290   5 4995

ISBN: 0-7643-1829-2